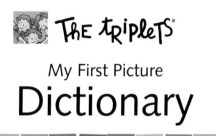

THE TRIPLETS

My First Picture
Dictionary

Spanish-English

Illustrations: From the original drawings of Roser Capdevila
Text: Isabel Carril

CONTENTS

My First Picture
Dictionary

Spanish-English

This picture dictionary introduces children to the marvellous world of words with colourful illustrations and simple translations.

Words are the key to a child's understanding of the world, and a sound acquisition of first words lays the foundations of successful language learning.

Learning is kept fun as children are guided through the pages of this picture dictionary by recurrent characters – young triplets. Children acquire new vocabulary and use their skills of observation, while they get to know the triplets' family, friends and school.

Parents can also suggest games to play, from searching for individual objects as well as the triplets in the larger illustrations, to answering the questions asked in the first and final pages of each chapter.

The games on the opening spread of each chapter are designed to introduce children to the chapter's theme. For example, in Family and friends, readers search the illustration for characters with particular attributes: tall, short, blond...

In the last spread of each chapter, words are introduced to explain how they are used to form sentences. For example, the final spread of Family and friends features words related to the expression "Who is it?" and "What are they doing?". Children can respond to these questions out loud, search for answers in the big illustrations throughout the chapter, and even use them to construct their own sentences.

Children will really enjoy expanding their vocabulary with this picture dictionary – and parents and teachers can join them in exploring the fascinating world of words.

La familia y los amigos
Family and friends

Busca a alguien que sea...
Find someone who is...

ALTO
TALL

BAJO
SHORT

GRUESO
STOUT

DELGADO
THIN

Busca a alguien que tenga...
Find someone who has...

PELO RUBIO
BLOND HAIR

PELO MORENO
DARK HAIR

PELO LARGO
LONG HAIR

PELO CORTO
SHORT HAIR

PELO LISO
STRAIGHT HAIR

PELO RIZADO
CURLY HAIR

Nuestra familia
Our family

ABUELO
GRANDFATHER

ABUELA
GRANDMOTHER

PADRE
FATHER

MADRE
MOTHER

HIJO
SON

HIJA
DAUGHTER

HERMANOS
BROTHERS

HERMANA
SISTER

NIETO
GRANDSON

NIETA
GRANDDAUGHTER

PRIMO
COUSIN

PRIMA
COUSIN

BEBÉ
BABY

MELLIZAS
TWINS

XILOFÓN
XYLOPHONE

PANDERETA
TAMBOURINE

PIANO
PIANO

VIOLÍN
VIOLIN

TROMPETA
TRUMPET

GUITARRA
GUITAR

TAMBOR
DRUM

BOMBILLA
BULB

ABURRIDA
BORED

DIVERTIDO
FUNNY

TRISTE
SAD

ALEGRE
HAPPY

CANSADO
TIRED

CONFETI
CONFETTI

Nuestros amigos
Our friends

PISCINA DE BOLAS
BALL POOL

BOLOS
SKITTLES

PARCHÍS
LUDO

PUZLE
JIGSAW PUZZLE

TÍTERE
PUPPET

VELAS
CANDLES

PATINETE
SCOOTER

BOLLOS
BUNS

CONSTRUCCIONES
BUILDING BLOCKS

CARTAS
CARDS

CASTILLO
CASTLE

MONOPATÍN
SKATEBOARD

JUEGO ELECTRÓNICO
COMPUTER GAME

MUÑECOS
DOLLS

REFRESCOS
SOFT DRINKS

ROBOT
ROBOT

GLOBO
BALLOON

TRICICLO
TRICYCLE

AMIGOS
FRIENDS

DISFRAZ
FANCY DRESS

DESCALZO
BAREFOOT

CALZADO
WEARING SHOES

BARCO PIRATA
PIRATE SHIP

BANDERA
FLAG

TARTA
CAKE

COCINITA
TOY KITCHEN

LIMPIO
CLEAN

SUCIO
DIRTY

La familia y los amigos
Family and friends

TÍO
UNCLE

TÍA
AUNT

SOBRINO
NEPHEW

SOBRINA
NIECE

BESAR
TO KISS

LEER
TO READ

HABLAR
TO TALK

GRITAR
TO SHOUT

ABRAZAR
TO HUG

¿Quién es?
Who is it?

¿Qué hacen?
What do they do?

ACARICIAR
TO CARESS

APLAUDIR
TO APPLAUD

BAILAR
TO DANCE

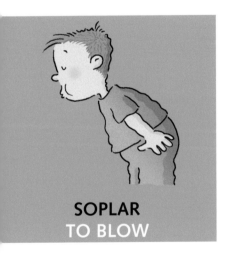

SOPLAR
TO BLOW

CAERSE
TO FALL

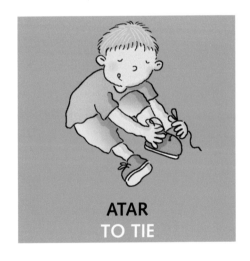

ATAR
TO TIE

BOSTEZAR
TO YAWN

CANTAR
TO SING

ESCUCHAR
TO LISTEN

La casa
The house

¿Dónde está cada dibujo?
Where is each picture?

¿Está a la derecha o a la izquierda de las Tres Mellizas?
Is it to the right or to the left of the triplets?

VENTANA
WINDOW

PERSIANA
BLIND

BALCÓN
BALCONY

CHIMENEA
CHIMNEY

VECINO
NEIGHBOUR

PUERTA
DOOR

TUBERÍA
PIPE

VALLA
FENCE

ESCALERA
STEPS

Nuestro salón comedor
Our dining-living room

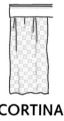

CORTINA
CURTAIN

LIBRO
BOOK

LÁMPARA
LAMP

MANTEL
TABLECLOTH

SERVILLETA
NAPKIN

COPA
GLASS

LIBRERÍA
BOOKSHELF

JARRÓN
VASE

SILLÓN
ARMCHAIR

DVD
DVD

VISILLO
NET CURTAIN

CUADRO
PICTURE

TELEVISIÓN
TELEVISION

SOFÁ
SOFA

ENCHUFE
PLUG

JARRA
JUG

ALFOMBRA
RUG

MINICADENA
HI-FI

PLATO
PLATE

TELÉFONO
TELEPHONE

SUELO
FLOOR

CUCHILLO
KNIFE

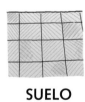

TENEDOR
FORK

BOTELLA
BOTTLE

RELOJ
CLOCK

ALTAVOZ
SPEAKER

SALERO
SALTCELLAR

TECHO
CEILING

Nuestro dormitorio
Our bedroom

FALDA
SKIRT

BRAGAS
KNICKERS

EDREDÓN
EIDERDOWN

CAJÓN
DRAWER

CHAQUETA
JACKET

BATA
DRESSING GOWN

PIJAMA
PYJAMAS

CAMISÓN
NIGHTDRESS

LITERAS
BUNK BEDS

JERSEY
JUMPER

VESTIDO
DRESS

ARMARIO
WARDROBE

ESCRITORIO
DESK

CALZONCILLOS
UNDERPANTS

CUNA
COT

CALCETINES
SOCKS

MANTA
BLANKET

CREMALLERA
ZIP

BOTÓN
BUTTON

PANTALÓN
TROUSERS

CAMISETA
T-SHIRT

PERCHA
HANGER

BOTAS
BOOTS

DEPORTIVAS
TRAINERS

ZAPATILLAS
SLIPPERS

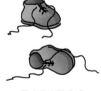

ZAPATOS
SHOES

SÁBANA
SHEET

ALMOHADA
PILLOW

Nuestra cocina
Our kitchen

COCINA
COOKER

BANDEJA
TRAY

SARTÉN
FRYING PAN

NEVERA
FRIDGE

CARNE
MEAT

PESCADO
FISH

FRUTAS
FRUIT

ESCURRIDOR
COLANDER

AZUCARERO
SUGAR BOWL

YOGUR
YOGURT

HORNO
OVEN

MICROONDAS
MICROWAVE

CUBO DE BASURA
RUBBISH BIN

CAFETERA
COFFEE POT

OLLA
POT

ESCOBA
BRUSH

FREGADERO
SINK

GRIFO
TAP

LAVAPLATOS
DISHWASHER

CONGELADOR
FREEZER

LAVADORA
WASHING MACHINE

VERDURAS
VEGETABLES

LECHE
MILK

CEREALES
CEREAL

CHOCOLATE
CHOCOLATE

PAN
BREAD

GALLETA
BISCUIT

ZUMO
JUICE

Nuestro cuarto de baño
Our bathroom

BRAZO
ARM

CODO
ELBOW

MANO
HAND

DEDO
FINGER

RODILLA
KNEE

HOMBRO
SHOULDER

PECHO
BREAST

ESPALDA
BACK

PIERNA
LEG

PIE
FOOT

TOBILLO
ANKLE

CULO
BOTTOM

FRENTE
FOREHEAD

OJO
EYE

20

PAPEL HIGIÉNICO
TOILET PAPER

DENTÍFRICO
TOOTHPASTE

LAVABO
WASHBASIN

VÁTER
TOILET

ESPONJA
SPONGE

JABÓN
SOAP

TOALLERO
TOWEL RACK

BAÑERA
BATH

NARIZ
NOSE

OREJA
EAR

BOCA
MOUTH

DIENTES
TEETH

LENGUA
TONGUE

CUELLO
NECK

La casa
The house

PEINE
COMB

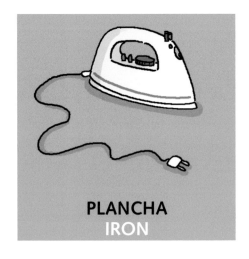

PLANCHA
IRON

DUCHA
SHOWER

CUCHARA
SPOON

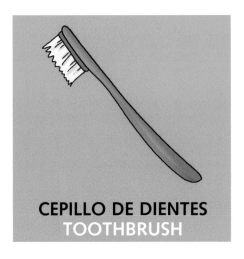

CEPILLO DE DIENTES
TOOTHBRUSH

ESPEJO
MIRROR

CAMA
BED

VASO
GLASS

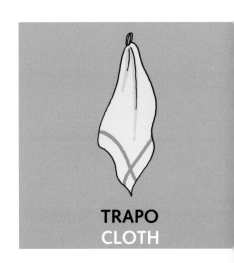

TRAPO
CLOTH

¿Qué es?
What is it?

¿Para qué sirve?
What is it used for?

PEINARSE
TO COMB

PLANCHAR
TO IRON

DUCHARSE
TO TAKE A SHOWER

COMER
TO EAT

LAVARSE LOS DIENTES
TO BRUSH YOUR TEETH

MIRARSE
TO LOOK AT YOURSELF

DORMIR
TO SLEEP

BEBER
TO DRINK

LIMPIAR
TO CLEAN

La escuela
The school

Veo, veo… una cosita… ¿De qué color?
¡Amarillo! ¿Qué es? ¡Un pollito!

I spy, I spy… Something… What colour is it?
Yellow! What is it? A chick!

AMARILLO
YELLOW

AZUL
BLUE

ROJO
RED

VERDE
GREEN

NARANJA
ORANGE

MARRÓN
BROWN

MORADO
PURPLE

BLANCO
WHITE

NEGRO
BLACK

Nuestra clase
Our classroom

ORDENADOR
COMPUTER

BORRADOR
DUSTER

GOMA
ERASER

PUNZÓN
BURIN

TIZA
CHALK

ESTUCHE
PENCIL CASE

JAULA
CAGE

HOJA
SHEET OF PAPER

PEGAMENTO
GLUE STICK

BABI
BIB

BOLÍGRAFO
PEN

SILLA
CHAIR

CERA
WAX CRAYONS

HÁMSTER
HAMSTER

CUADERNO
NOTEBOOK

MURAL
MURAL

MESA
TABLE

PINCEL
PAINTBRUSH

SACAPUNTAS
PENCIL
SHARPENER

PINTURAS
PAINTS

PECERA
FISHTANK

PIZARRA
BLACKBOARD

LÁPIZ
PENCIL

CARPETA
FOLDER

PLASTILINA
MODELLING PASTE

REGLA
RULER

TIJERAS
SCISSORS

ESTANTERÍA
SHELF

Nuestro patio
Our playground

PELOTA
BALL

BOCADILLO
SANDWICH

FUENTE
FOUNTAIN

BANCO
BENCH

COLUMPIOS
SWINGS

PORTERÍA
GOALPOST

TOBOGÁN
SLIDE

PEONZA
SPINNING TOP

PITO
WHISTLE

CANICAS
MARBLES

AGUA
WATER

ÁRBOL
TREE

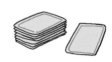

CROMOS
PICTURE CARDS

YOYÓ
YO-YO

AVIÓN DE PAPEL
PAPER PLANE

MOCHILA
BACKPACK

RASTRILLO
RAKE

HOJAS
LEAVES

ARENA
SAND

CUERDA DE SALTAR
SKIPPING ROPE

GUANTES
GLOVES

LAZO
BOW

PALA
SHOVEL

PAJARITO
LITTLE BIRD

MACETA
FLOWERPOT

CUBO
BUCKET

AROS
HOOPS

GAFAS
GLASSES

La escuela
The school

PROFESORA
TEACHER

ÁRBITRO
REFEREE

PORTERA
GOALKEEPER

SALTAR
TO JUMP

LLORAR
TO CRY

REÍR
TO LAUGH

BOTAR
TO BOUNCE

SUBIR
TO GO UP

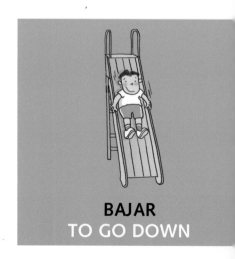

BAJAR
TO GO DOWN

¿Qué hacen?
What do they do?

¿Cómo están?
How are they?

¿Dónde está?
Where is it?

LANZAR
TO THROW

CORRER
TO RUN

DE PIE
STANDING

SENTADO
SITTING

DE RODILLAS
ON YOUR KNEES

ARRIBA
UP

ABAJO
DOWN

DENTRO
INSIDE

FUERA
OUTSIDE

La ciudad
The city

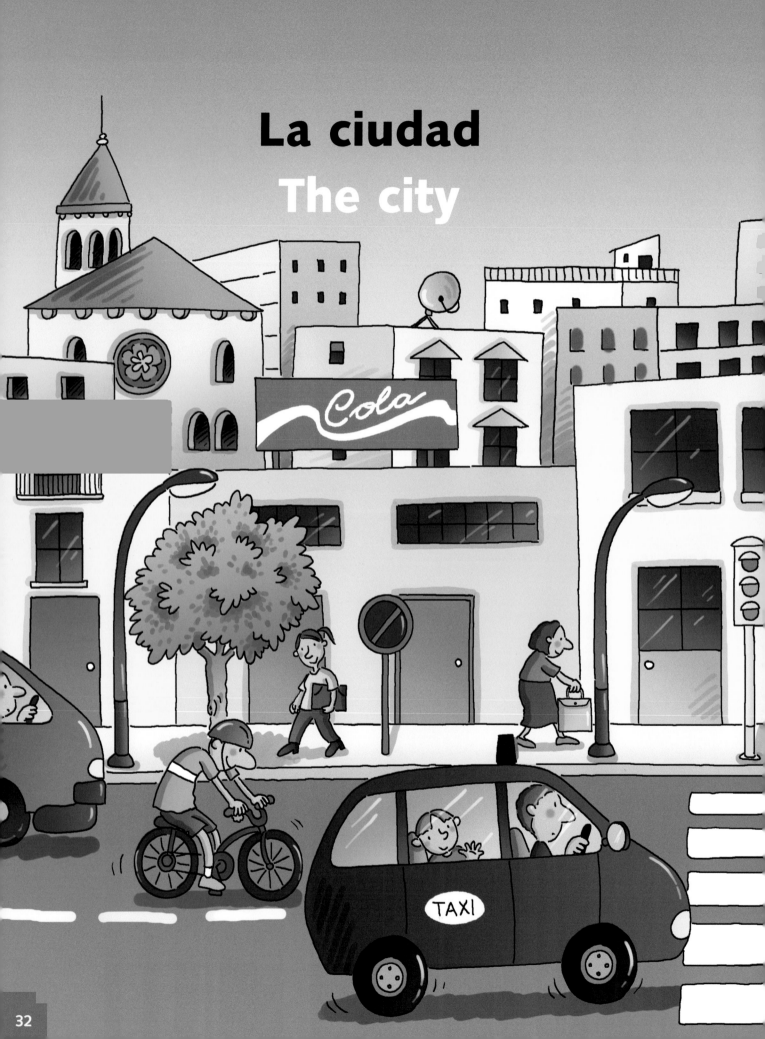

Busca en la ilustración estas formas:
Find these shapes in the picture:

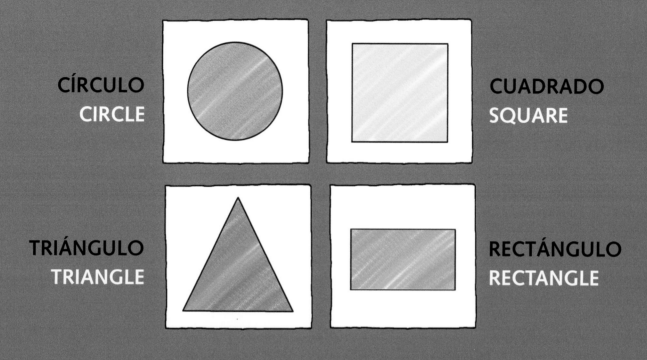

CÍRCULO
CIRCLE

CUADRADO
SQUARE

TRIÁNGULO
TRIANGLE

RECTÁNGULO
RECTANGLE

¿Qué forma tienen...?
What is the shape of a...?

TEJADO
ROOF

RUEDA
WHEEL

CARTEL
SIGN

BOLSO
BAG

Nuestra calle
Our street

EDIFICIO
BUILDING

BANCO
BANK

**PASO
DE CEBRA**
ZEBRA
CROSSING

ACERA
PAVEMENT

CALZADA
ROAD

RASCACIELOS
SKYSCRAPER

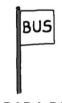

**PARADA DE
AUTOBÚS**
BUS STOP

TIENDA
SHOP

IGLESIA
CHURCH

CAMPANA
BELL

SEMÁFORO
TRAFFIC LIGHTS

FAROLA
STREET LAMP

TOLDO
AWNING

RESTAURANTE
RESTAURANT

PARQUE
PARK

MONUMENTO
MONUMENT

CABINA TELEFÓNICA
PHONE BOX

ALCANTARILLA
SEWER

BUZÓN
POSTBOX

HOTEL
HOTEL

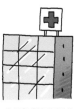

HOSPITAL
HOSPITAL

SEÑAL DE TRÁFICO
TRAFFIC SIGN

CONDUCTOR
DRIVER

PEATÓN
PEDESTRIAN

AYUNTAMIENTO
TOWN HALL

TEATRO
THEATRE

BIBLIOTECA
LIBRARY

CINE
CINEMA

El viaje
The trip

COCHE
CAR

MOTO
MOTORBIKE

COCHE DE BOMBEROS
FIRE ENGINE

VOLANTE
STEERING WHEEL

BICICLETA
BICYCLE

CASCO
HELMET

MANILLAR
HANDLEBARS

SILLÍN
SADDLE

APARCAMIENTO
CAR PARK

MALETA
SUITCASE

AVIÓN
AEROPLANE

TREN
TRAIN

BARCO
SHIP

METRO
UNDERGROUND

AMBULANCIA
AMBULANCE

AUTOBÚS
BUS

TAXI
TAXI

GRÚA
CRANE

HELICÓPTERO
HELICOPTER

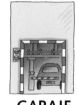

GARAJE
GARAGE

FURGONETA
VAN

CINTURÓN DE SEGURIDAD
SEAT BELT

PEDAL
PEDAL

VAGÓN
CARRIAGE

VENTANILLA
WINDOW

CARRETERA
HIGHWAY

MAQUINISTA
TRAIN DRIVER

CAMIÓN
LORRY

¿Qué nos gustaría ser de mayores?
What would you like to do when you

ARQUITECTO
ARCHITECT

BASURERO
REFUSE
COLLECTOR

PORTERO
CONCIERGE

CARTERA
POSTWOMAN

INFORMÁTICO
IT SPECIALIST

DETECTIVE
DETECTIVE

FARMACÉUTICA
PHARMACIST

PELUQUERA
HAIRDRESSER

CAMARERO
WAITER

TENDERA
SHOPKEEPER

w up?

PINTOR
PAINTER

ESCRITORA
WRITER

JARDINERA
GARDENER

BARRENDERO
STREET
SWEEPER

BAILARINA
DANCER

COCINERA
COOK

POLICÍA
POLICEMAN

MECÁNICO
MECHANIC

FOTÓGRAFA
PHOTOGRAPHER

ENFERMERA
NURSE

MÉDICO
DOCTOR

COMERCIAL
SALESMAN

ACTRIZ
ACTRESS

PERIODISTA
JOURNALIST

MÚSICO
MUSICIAN

CIENTÍFICA
SCIENTIST

CANTANTE
SINGER

TAXISTA
TAXI DRIVER

Los deportes
Sports

SALTO DE ALTURA
HIGH JUMP

SALTO DE LONGITUD
LONG JUMP

SALTO DE VALLAS
HURDLES

CINTA DE GIMNASIA
GYMNASTICS RIBBON

PATINAJE SOBRE HIELO
ICE SKATING

PATINAJE SOBRE RUEDAS
ROLLER SKATING

CESTA DE BALONCESTO
BASKET

GORRO DE PISCINA
SWIMMING CAP

BALONCESTO
BASKETBALL

CHANCLETAS
FLIP-FLOPS

CHÁNDAL
TRACKSUIT

COLCHONETA
MAT

FÚTBOL
FOOTBALL

GIMNASIA
GYMNASTICS

HACER LA VOLTERETA
SOMERSAULT

HACER EL PINO
HANDSTAND

RODILLERAS
KNEE PADS

TENIS
TENNIS

PATÍN
ROLLER SKATE

VOLEY-PLAYA
BEACH VOLLEYBALL

PING-PONG
PING-PONG

BAÑADOR
SWIMSUIT

JUDO
JUDO

JUGADOR
PLAYER

MAILLOT
LEOTARD

NATACIÓN
SWIMMING

RED
NET

RAQUETA
RACKET

La ciudad
The city

ESPERAR EL AUTOBÚS
TO WAIT FOR THE BUS

LLAMAR POR TELÉFONO
TO MAKE A PHONE CALL

CRUZAR
TO CROSS

CONDUCIR
TO DRIVE

APARCAR
TO PARK

NAVEGAR
TO SAIL

IR EN TREN
TO GO BY TRAIN

MONTAR EN BICI
TO RIDE A BICYCLE

SEÑALAR
TO POINT

...cuando viajamos?

...when we travel?

...cuando practicamos deporte?

...when we play sports?

...cuando ya somos mayores?

...when we are adults?

ENCESTAR
TO SCORE

DESCANSAR
TO REST

SUDAR
TO SWEAT

CHUTAR
TO SHOOT

PITAR
TO BLOW A WHISTLE

TRABAJAR
TO WORK

CURAR
TO CURE

INVESTIGAR
TO INVESTIGATE

COCINAR
TO COOK

Animales y plantas
Animals and plants

UNO
ONE

DOS
TWO

TRES
THREE

CUATRO
FOUR

CINCO
FIVE

SEIS
SIX

SIETE
SEVEN

OCHO
EIGHT

NUEVE
NINE

DIEZ
TEN

¿Cuántos hay?
How many are there?

ARDILLA
SQUIRREL

RATÓN
MOUSE

LAGARTIJA
LIZARD

MARIPOSA
BUTTERFLY

MARIQUITA
LADYBIRD

PINO
PINE

ROSA
ROSE

TULIPÁN
TULIP

MARGARITA
DAISY

LILA
LILAC

Vamos a la granja
Let's go to the farm

GALLINA
HEN

CABALLO
HORSE

CABRA
GOAT

GALLO
COCK

TRACTOR
TRACTOR

REGADERA
WATERING CAN

AZADA
HOE

CARRETILLA
WHEELBARROW

GRANJERO
FARMER

CHARCA
POND

POLLITO
CHICK

PATO
DUCK

CERDO
PIG

BURRO
DONKEY

CONEJO
RABBIT

OVEJA
SHEEP

VACA
COW

RANA
FROG

PAVO
TURKEY

GATO
CAT

CORDERO
LAMB

CAMPO DE CULTIVO
PLOUGHED FIELD

PAJAR
HAYLOFT

HUERTO
VEGETABLE GARDEN

OCA
GOOSE

POCILGA
PIGSTY

CORRAL
FARMYARD

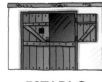

ESTABLO
STABLE

Vamos al zoo
Let's go to the zoo

LEÓN
LION

LEOPARDO
LEOPARD

OSO PARDO
BROWN BEAR

OSO POLAR
POLAR BEAR

PANTERA
PANTHER

TIGRE
TIGER

RENO
REINDEER

ELEFANTE
ELEPHANT

RINOCERONTE
RHINO

GORILA
GORILLA

HIPOPÓTAMO
HIPPO

CEBRA
ZEBRA

JIRAFA
GIRAFFE

OSO PANDA
PANDA BEAR

KOALA
KOALA

MONO
MONKEY

ÁGUILA
EAGLE

BUITRE
VULTURE

NIDO
NEST

CIGÜEÑA
STORK

BÚHO
OWL

LORO
PARROT

CANGURO
KANGAROO

PINGÜINO
PENGUIN

CAMELLO
CAMEL

SERPIENTE
SNAKE

PALOMA
PIGEON

GORRIÓN
SPARROW

Vamos al acuario
Let's go to the aquarium

TIBURÓN
SHARK

MORENA
MORAY

RAYA
RAYFISH

PEZ PAYASO
CLOWNFISH

TORTUGA
TORTOISE

ESTRELLA DE MAR
STARFISH

ERIZO
SEA URCHIN

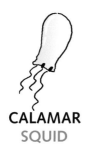

CALAMAR
SQUID

PULPO
OCTOPUS

MEDUSA
JELLYFISH

MEJILLÓN
MUSSEL

MERLUZA
HAKE

LENGUADO
SOLE

ALGA
SEA WEED

CANGREJO
CRAB

SARDINA
SARDINE

LANGOSTA
LOBSTER

ALMEJA
CLAM

BACALAO
COD

BÍGARO
WINKLE

GAMBA
PRAWN

LAPA
LIMPET

LOBO MARINO
SEAL

ORCA
KILLER WHALE

DELFÍN
DOLPHIN

FOCA
SEAL

BALLENA
WHALE

MORSA
WALRUS

Animales y plantas
Animals and plants

HOMBRE
MAN

MUJER
WOMAN

PERRO
DOG

PEZ
FISH

ASOMARSE
TO LEAN OUT

SEMBRAR
TO SOW

NADAR
TO SWIM

ENTRAR
TO GO IN

SALIR
TO GO OUT

¿Quién es?
Who is it?

¿Qué animal es?
What animal is it?

¿Qué hacen?
What do they do?

ABRIR
TO OPEN

CERRAR
TO CLOSE

ALIMENTAR
TO FEED

VOLAR
TO FLY

SALUDAR
TO SAY HELLO

LADRAR
TO BARK

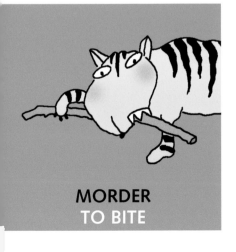

MORDER
TO BITE

TREPAR
TO CLIMB

PASEAR
TO TAKE A STROLL

CASTELLANO

ENGLISH

A B C D E F G H I J K L M N Ñ O P Q R S T U V W X Y Z

A
B
C
D
E
F
G
H
I
J
K
L
M
N
Ñ
O
P
Q
R
S
T
U
V
W
X
Y
Z

A
B
C
D
E
F
G
H
I
J
K
L
M
N
Ñ
O
P
Q
R
S
T
U
V
W
X
Y
Z

A
B
C
D
E
F
G
H
I
J
K
L
M
N
Ñ
O
P
Q
R
S
T
U
V
W
X
Y
Z

A
B
C
D
E
F
G
H
I
J
K
L
M
N
Ñ
O
P
Q
R
S
T
U
V
W
X
Y
Z

First published in the UK in 2008 by Wayland

© Cromosoma, SA y Televisió de Catalunya, 2008
© Grupo Editorial Bruño, S.L., 2008

Wayland
338 Euston Road
London NW1 3BH

Wayland Australia
Level 17/207 Kent Street
Sydney NSW 2000

Illustrations: from the original drawings of Roser Capdevila
Text: Isabel Carril
Translation into English: John Liddy

ISBN 9780750256940
ISBN Cromosoma:978-84-92419-18-0

Wayland is a division of Hachette Children's Books,
an Hachette Livre UK company.